OXFORD

Read at Home

First Dictionary

Illustrations by Alex Brychta
Main Consultant Roderick Hunt
Text compiled by Clare Kirtley

OXFORD
UNIVERSITY PRESS

KT-155-415

Introduction

This First Dictionary introduces children to the important features of a dictionary. It contains over 300 words, each word in the A to Z section being in alphabetical order with a simple definition and an interesting, colourful picture.

The words in the dictionary have been carefully chosen to support and develop children's reading, writing and speaking ability.

Here are the main features on the A to Z pages:

alphabet

capital letter

letter

symbol for verb

picture

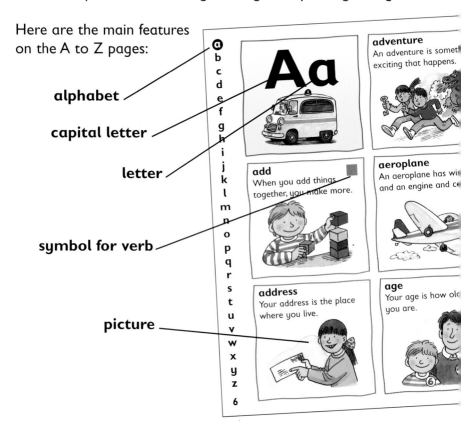

Aa

adventure
An adventure is somet[hing] exciting that happens.

add
When you add things together, you make more.

aeroplane
An aeroplane has wi[ngs] and an engine and c[...]

address
Your address is the place where you live.

age
Your age is how old you are.

a b c d e f g h i j k l m n o p q r s t u v w x y z

6

The first Dictionary supports children's reading and helps children to acquire basic dictionary and reference skills in an enjoyable way. They can learn about the alphabet and alphabetical order, they can find out how to locate a word by using the initial letter, they can check their own spelling, and they can learn how to use simple definitions of words and so extend their vocabulary.

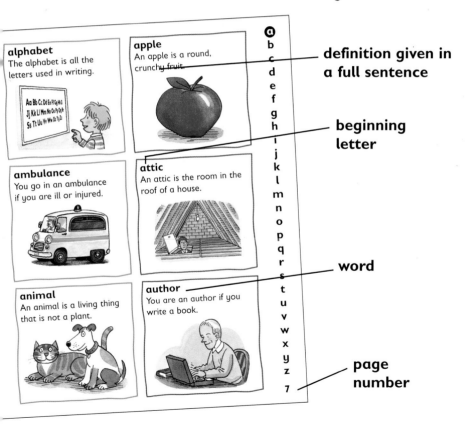

alphabet
The alphabet is all the letters used in writing.

apple
An apple is a round, crunchy fruit.

definition given in a full sentence

beginning letter

ambulance
You go in an ambulance if you are ill or injured.

attic
An attic is the room in the roof of a house.

animal
An animal is a living thing that is not a plant.

author
You are an author if you write a book.

word

page number

a
b
c
d
e
f
g
h
i
j
k
l
m
n
o
p
q
r
s
t
u
v
w
x
y
z

7

Aa

adventure

An adventure is something exciting that happens.

add

When you add things together, you make more.

aeroplane

An aeroplane has wings and an engine and can fly.

address

Your address is the place where you live.

age

Your age is how old you are.

alphabet
The alphabet is all the letters used in writing.

apple
An apple is a round, crunchy fruit.

ambulance
You go in an ambulance if you are ill or injured.

attic
An attic is the room in the roof of a house.

animal
An animal is a living thing that is not a plant.

author
You are an author if you write a book.

Bb

balloon

A balloon is made from rubber. You blow it up.

baby

A baby is a very young child.

bark

A dog barks. It is a loud sound.

ball

A ball is round. You can play games with it.

bed

You sleep in a bed.

bedroom
A bedroom is a room you sleep in.

bird
A bird is an animal with wings, feathers and a beak.

bicycle
A bicycle has two wheels and you ride on it.

birthday
Your birthday is the day you were born.

big
An elephant is big to you.

boat
A boat floats on water.

book
A book has pages and a cover.

bridge
A bridge goes over a river, railway or road.

bounce
When you bounce a ball, it comes back up again.

bus
A bus takes people where they want to go.

box
A box holds things. It is often made from cardboard.

butterfly
A butterfly is an insect with four large wings.

Cc

castle
A castle is a large old building with thick walls.

cake
A cake is a sweet food.

cat
A cat is a small furry animal.

car
A car has wheels and an engine.

chair
You sit on a chair.

climb
When you climb, you go up or down something.

computer
A computer stores information.

clown
A clown is someone who makes you laugh.

cook
You cook food by heating it.

coat
You wear a coat over your clothes when you go outside.

cross
If you are cross, you feel angry.

Dd

dog
A dog is an animal you can keep as a pet.

dance
When you dance, you move to music.

doll
A doll is a toy person.

day
You are awake during the day.

dolphin
A dolphin is an animal that lives in the sea.

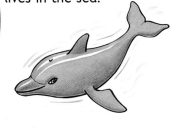

door
You open a door to go into a room.

dream
When you dream, you see and hear things in your sleep.

dragon
A dragon is a fierce monster in stories.

drink
You can drink milk.

draw
You draw a picture with a pencil, pen or crayon.

drum
A drum makes a banging noise when you beat it.

Ee

egg
An egg has a thin hard shell.

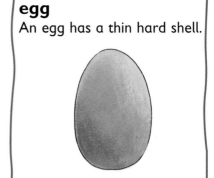

ear
You use your ears to hear.

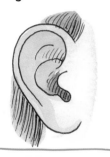

elephant
An elephant is a large animal with a trunk.

eat
You need to eat food to live.

eye
You use your eyes to see.

Ff

farm
A farm is where food is grown.

fair
You have fun at a fair.

feather
Birds have feathers instead of fur or hair.

fall
When you fall over, you hit the ground.

find
You need to look for something to find it.

fire
A fire is something burning.
It is hot and bright.

flower
A flower is part of a plant.

fire engine
A fire engine is a lorry that
is used to put out fires.

food
Food is what you eat to
grow.

fish
A fish is an animal that lives
under water.

frog
A frog is an animal with
wet skin and webbed feet.

a
b
c
d
e
f
g
h
i
j
k
l
m
n
o
p
q
r
s
t
u
v
w
x
y
z

18

Gg

garden
You grow flowers and vegetables in a garden.

game
You play a game.

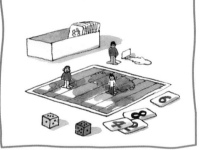

giant
If something is giant, it is very big.

garage
A car is kept in a garage.

giraffe
A giraffe is an animal with a long neck.

glasses
You wear glasses to help you see better.

goldfish
A goldfish is a small orange fish.

glow
When something glows, it gives off light and heat.

good
When you are good, people like you.

go-kart
A go-kart has four wheels and you ride on it.

guitar
A guitar is an instrument with strings.

a
b
c
d
e
f
g
h
i
j
k
l
m
n
o
p
q
r
s
t
u
v
w
x
y
z

20

Hh

happy
When you are happy, you feel good.

hair
Your hair grows on your head.

hat
You wear a hat on your head.

hand
Your hand has four fingers and a thumb.

head
Your eyes, ears and nose are on your head.

helicopter
A helicopter has blades that spin round on top.

hot
If something is hot, it can burn you.

holiday
A holiday is when you do not go to school or work.

house
You can live in a house.

hospital
You go to hospital if you are ill.

hungry
If you are hungry, you want to eat.

a
b
c
d
e
f
g
h
i
j
k
l
m
n
o
p
q
r
s
t
u
v
w
x
y
z

22

idea
If you have an idea, you think of something.

ice
Freezing water turns to ice.

insect
An insect is a small animal with six legs.

ice cream
Ice cream is a very cold food that tastes like cream.

instrument
You use an instrument to make music.

Jj

journey
You travel from place to place on a journey.

jam
You make jam from fruit and sugar.

jug
You use a jug to pour a drink.

joke
A joke is a story that makes you laugh.

jump
When you jump, you go up into the air.

Kk

king
Some countries are ruled by a king.

kettle
You use a kettle to boil water.

kitchen
You cook in a kitchen.

key
You use a key to unlock a door.

kite
A kite flies in the air at the end of a long string.

Ll

leaf
A leaf grows on a plant.

ladder
A ladder has rungs you can climb up and down.

letter
You write a letter to tell someone something.

Dear Wilf,
Please come to my party on Sunday.
Love, Biff

laugh
You laugh when something is funny.

library
Books are kept in a library.

a
b
c
d
e
f
g
h
i
j
k
l
m
n
o
p
q
r
s
t
u
v
w
x
y
z

26

light
You need light to see. Light comes from a lamp.

lock
A lock has a key to keep doors safely shut.

like
If you like someone, you think they are nice.

look
You use your eyes to look.

little
A mouse is little to you.

lose
If you lose something, you can not find it.

Mm

map
A map shows you how to get to places.

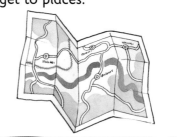

magic
Magic makes impossible things happen.

mend
You mend something which is broken.

make
You make something by putting things together.

milk
You can drink cow's milk.

a
b
c
d
e
f
g
h
i
j
k
l
m
n
o
p
q
r
s
t
u
v
w
x
y
z

mirror

You look at yourself in a mirror.

moon

You often see the moon in the sky at night.

money

You use money to buy things.

mountain

A mountain is a high hill.

monkey

A monkey is a furry animal that lives in trees.

mouse

A mouse is a small animal with a long tail.

Nn

new
Something is new when you first get it.

name
Your name is what people call you.

night
It is dark at night time.

nest
A bird lives in a nest.

nose
You use your nose to smell.

Oo

open
You open a door.

octopus
An octopus is a sea creature with eight arms.

orange
An orange is a round fruit with thick peel.

old
You are old if you were born a long time ago.

owl
An owl is a bird which flies at night.

Pp

pair
A pair is two things which go together.

page
A page is part of a book.

park
You can play in a park.

paint
You paint with a brush to colour a picture.

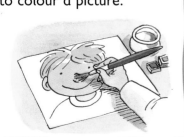

party
You have fun at a party with your friends.

pencil
You use a pencil to write or draw.

pool
A pool has water in it.

photograph
You take a photograph with a camera.

pull
You can pull with your arms.

play
When you play, you have fun.

push
You push a wheelbarrow.

Qq

queue
You line up in a queue to wait for a bus.

queen
A queen is a woman who rules a country.

quick
You are quick when you move fast.

question
You ask a question to find out something.

quiet
You are quiet when you make very little noise.

a
b
c
d
e
f
g
h
i
j
k
l
m
n
o
p
q
r
s
t
u
v
w
x
y
z

Rr

rain
The rain is water falling from the sky.

rabbit
A rabbit is a small animal with long ears.

read
You read words written in books or on signs.

race
You run a race to find out who is the fastest.

recorder
A recorder is an instrument that you blow.

ride
You can ride a bicycle.

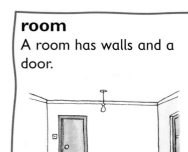

room
A room has walls and a door.

river
A river is a large stream of water.

rope
A rope is used to tie and pull things.

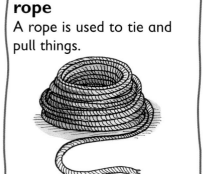

rocket
A rocket sends spacecraft into space.

run
When you run, you move your legs quickly.

Ss

sandwich

A sandwich is two slices of bread with food between them.

sad

You are sad when you feel unhappy.

school

You go to school to learn.

sand

Sand is very fine bits of rock. You find it by the sea.

shop

You buy things in a shop.

sleep
When you sleep, you close your eyes and rest.

story
A story is a made up adventure. You read stories in books.

snow
Snow is frozen rain that falls from the sky.

stream
A stream is a small river.

storm
A storm is a strong wind with rain or snow.

swing
A swing is a seat that moves backwards and forwards.

Tt

teddy
A teddy is a soft toy bear.

table
You sit at a table.

television
You watch and listen to things on television.

teacher
A teacher is a person who helps you to learn.

tent
You can sleep outside in a tent.

throw
You throw a ball through the air.

toy
You play with a toy.

toboggan
A toboggan slides along on snow.

tray
You carry things on a tray.

tooth
You use your teeth to bite and chew your food. A tooth can fall out.

tree
A tree is a tall plant with leaves.

a
b
c
d
e
f
g
h
i
j
k
l
m
n
o
p
q
r
s
t
u
v
w
x
y
z

Uu

uniform
The police and nurses wear a uniform.

ugly
If something is ugly, it is not nice to look at.

upset
When you are upset, you are not happy.

umbrella
An umbrella keeps you dry when it rains.

use
You use tools to make things.

Vv

vase
You put flowers in a vase.

van
A van can carry lots of things.

vegetable
A vegetable is a plant that you can eat.

vanish
If you vanish, you disappear.

video
A video records sound and pictures from the television.

Ww

water
Rivers and seas are made up of water.

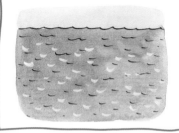

wall
A wall is made of brick or stone.

weather
Snow, rain and sunshine are types of weather.

wash
You wash with soap and water to get clean.

wheel
A wheel turns round and round.

wind
The wind is air moving.

wood
A wood is where a group of trees grow.

window
A window is a space in a wall to let in light.

word
You use words when you speak or write.

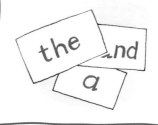

witch
A witch can do magic.

write
You write words for others to read.

Xx

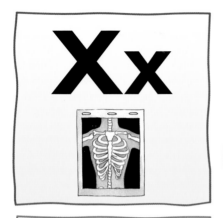

Yy

X-ray
An X-ray shows the inside of your body.

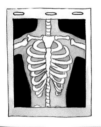

yawn
You yawn when you are tired.

xylophone
A xylophone is an instrument with wooden or metal bars.

year
There are twelve months in a year.

yell

When you yell, you shout loudly.

Zz

yogurt

You make yogurt from sour milk.

zebra

A zebra is an animal with black and white stripes.

young

You are young if you were born a short time ago.

zoo

You can see wild animals at a zoo.

a b c d e f g h i j k l m n o p q r s t u v w x **y z**

45

For Dylan and Kelly – AB
For Rosie – RH
For Rose, Amy and Eleanor – CK

OXFORD
UNIVERSITY PRESS
Great Clarendon Street, Oxford OX2 6DP

Oxford University Press is a department of the University of Oxford.
It furthers the University's objective of excellence in research, scholarship,
and education by publishing worldwide in

Oxford   New York

Auckland   Cape Town   Dar es Salaam   Hong Kong   Karachi
Kuala Lumpur   Madrid   Melbourne   Mexico City   Nairobi
New Delhi   Shanghai   Taipei   Toronto

With offices in

Argentina   Austria   Brazil   Chile   Czech Republic   France   Greece
Guatemala   Hungary   Italy   Japan   Poland   Portugal   Singapore
South Korea   Switzerland   Thailand   Turkey   Ukraine   Vietnam

Oxford is a registered trade mark of Oxford University Press
in the UK and in certain other countries

First published 2000 as the Oxford Reading Tree Dictionary

This edition 2006

ISBN-13: 978-0-19-911554-9

Large Format ISBN-13: 978-0-19-279227-3

3 5 7 9 10 8 6 4 2

Printed in China by Imago